Revolutionary Recipes

Colonial Food, Lore, & More

Patricia B. Mitchell

Copyright © 1988 by Patricia B. Mitchell.

Published 1988 by the author at the
Sims-Mitchell House Bed & Breakfast,
242 Whittle Street SW, P. O. Box 846,
Chatham, VA   24531

Printed in U. S. A.
ISBN 0-925117-07-2

Second Printing, February 1989

CONTENTS

Introduction 1

Breakfast. 3
    BUCKWHEAT CAKES 4
    CORN PONE 5
    CHICKEN (OR TURKEY) HASH. 6

Midday Meal. 7
    FRENCH ONION SOUP 8
    OYSTER STEW 9
    BAKED HAM 9
    CHICKEN POT PIE 9
    STRING BEANS. 12
    CORN PUDDING. 12
    SALLY LUNN. 13
    MARBLEHEAD PUDDING. 13
    STRAWBERRY PRESERVES. 14
    JUMBLES 15
    FUDGE 15
    LEMON CHEESECAKE. 16
    UPDATED CHEESECAKE. 16
    COTTAGE CHEESE PIE. 17
    APPLE BROWN BETTY 17
    APRICOT ICE CREAM 18
    SYLLABUB. 19
    WASSAIL 19
    20TH CENTURY NO-BAKE FRUIT CAKE 21

Supper 23
    LA MÉDIATRICE/PEACEMAKER/OYSTER LOAF FOR TWO. . . 23
    CRAB CAKES. 25

Footnotes. 27

INTRODUCTION

"Our greatest luxuries now consisted in a little water, stiffened with flour, in imitation of shoemakers' paste... In company was a poor dog... [who] became a prey for the sustenance of the assassinators. The poor animal was instantly devoured, without leaving any vestige of the sacrifice. Nor did the shaving soap, ... leather of [our] shoes, cartridge boxes, etc., share any better fate."[1]

So wrote Dr. Isaac Senter, one of Col. Benedict Arnold's troops (in the Continental Army) involved in the march to, and attack on, Quebec in 1775.

In the eight years of fighting for freedom, soldiers in the American Revolution often experienced food shortages, due largely to transportation problems, the tendency of citizens to hoard food, and the purposeful destruction of crops and food stores by Tories. However, because at peak strength Continental forces only numbered 20,000 of a population somewhat less than four million, there was food available. (Sometimes local citizens were actually unaware of the troops' lack, so foraging became necessary for the Continental soldier.)

Theoretically, the soldier was supplied ample nourishment. The Army around Boston, for example, issued each soldier the following daily ration:

> One pound of bread;
> Half a pound of beef and half a pound of pork; and if pork cannot be had, one pound and a quarter of beef; and one day in seven they shall have one pound and one quarter of salt fish, instead of one day's allowance of meat;
> One pint of milk, or if milk cannot be had, one gill of rice;
> One quart of good spruce or malt beer;
> One gill of peas or beans, or other sauce equivalent;
> Six ounces of good butter per week;
> One pound of good common soap for six men per week;
> Half a pint of vinegar per week per man, if it can be had.[2]

At Valley Forge the list of daily rations (obviously, listing it was not the same as delivering it) included:

One and a half pounds of flour or bread,
One pound of beef or fish, or three-fourths
    pound of pork, and
One gill of whiskey or spirits; or
One and a half pounds of flour,
Half pound of pork or bacon,
Half pint of peas or beans, and
One gill of whiskey or spirits.³

The purpose of this book is to explore how this fare compared to an 18th-century colonist's normal diet, to present several authentic pre-Revolutionary War recipes, and to give some modernized recipes which commemorate the food and events of the colonial era.

BREAKFAST

The colonial family of adequate means dined well. Breakfast was served between 9 and 10 a.m. The meal might include oatmeal or cornmeal mush; a choice of game (venison or bear steaks, for example), cold sliced ham, beefsteak, cold sliced roast mutton chops, veal cutlet, sausages, scrapple (in Pennsylvania and its derivative regions), poultry, chicken or turkey hash; occasionally eggs, which were usually boiled; perhaps fruit (although this was a rarity on the breakfast table); griddle cakes (buckwheat cakes and cornmeal cakes were popular); breads (in the North loaf bread was often baked the day before, and then served cut in thick slices with butter; in the South, freshly baked breads were typical: rolls, muffins, soda biscuits, beaten biscuits). The meal was accompanied by a selection of milk, coffee, tea, or chocolate.

Memories of such a bountiful meal must have filled the minds of many Continental officers and other well-to-do soldiers as they gathered in their units of 6 to 8 men to partake of the morning sustenance. Rations were usually issued uncooked, and a set of cooking utensils was issued for use among a group of 6 to as many as 12 men. Such a group or "mess" selected the best (or most willing) cooks in their number to cook for the rest. (In winter encampments, whole companies would occasionally go together and appoint cooks, but the small "mess" was the norm.)

Officers were issued kettles with covers; enlisted men got no lids. Each "mess" had one kettle. In the kettles men cooked peas, beans, soups, stews, and boiled meat. (The men were advised that provisions "ought always to be boiled or roasted, never fried, baked or broiled, which modes are very unhealthy.")[1]

The camp kettles were sometimes carried in horse-drawn wagons, and sometimes worn by the soldier over the shoulder in a linen carrying case with strap. The men also carried a plate or trencher, and a spoon, perhaps a multipurpose knife and a fork, and a cow horn cup in a haversack. The horn cup was used for whiskey or beer. The canteen was mostly used to carry water. (Each soldier was supposed to be issued his own canteen, but in 1778 Col. Charles C. Pinckney of Charleston bemoaned the cruelty of providing only one canteen for every 6 to 8 men. Since a canteen held only one quart of liquid, that equaled only four ounces of water per man for perhaps a whole day of marching -- very little water in the hot Southern climate.)[2]

High-ranking officers did not usually have to make do with the issue camp kettles, wooden trenchers, spoons, and knives which enlisted men and junior officers used. For example, the elaborate mess chest which Gen. George Washington carried with him in the field is now in the collection of the Smithsonian Institution in Washington, D. C. It is a compact, rectangular miniature trunk. In the top, fitted into the raised lid, are two pewter platters. The chest also holds six pewter plates; four pots (called kettles) with detachable wooden handles; a folding grill; eight bottles for spirits (alcoholic beverages); containers for seasonings; two knives and four forks; and two tinder boxes. In addition to the contents of this mess chest, orders exist for many more plates and canisters, so this neat trunk only held part of Washington's mess equipment.

We can speculate, though, that the average enlisted soldiers in their mess of 6-8 men had a rather limited menu, and at times, very frugal fare. The quality of the "cuisine" of course depended upon what rations were available to the selected cook, and his personal creativity and energy. Breakfast might have consisted of baked bread (which was at times issued to the troops); or perhaps the unpalatable fire cake, a chewy, soggy glob of flour paste which was baked on a stone. It contained no leavening and little if any salt. (This sad papier-mâché-like concoction was a Valley Forge specialty.) Perchance there was milk to drink or spirits, and some beans or meat or fish. Maybe foraging had turned up some potatoes. . . No doubt many a man thought longingly of a pretty, plump wife at home, her cheeks rosy from the fire as she prepared buckwheat cakes, corn pone, or hash for breakfast.

BUCKWHEAT PANCAKES

1 tbsp. yeast
1/4 c. warm water
1/2 tsp. salt
1-2 tbsp. honey or sugar

1 1/2 c. warm milk
2 or 3 eggs
1 tbsp. vegetable oil
1 c. whole wheat flour
1 c. buckwheat flour

    Dissolve yeast in warm water, with salt and sweetener added. Beat in remaining ingredients with a rotary beater. At this point, cover and let rise 30 or 40 minutes; or refrigerate overnight in a 3-quart container. (If refrigerated, let the batter come to room temperature before using in the morning.)

    Cook pancakes on a lightly greased griddle or in a skillet over medium-high heat (375° F.). Flip pancakes when small bubbles appear. Remove when they stop steaming. Makes about sixteen 4-inch pancakes.

CORN PONE

2 c. cornmeal
3/4 tsp. salt (or less)
Boiling water
2 tbsp. butter or margarine, melted;
    or vegetable oil

    Combine all ingredients to make a semi-stiff mush. Spread 1/4-inch thick in a well-greased heavy pan and bake at 375° F. 20 to 25 minutes. (Corn pones used to be baked on a greased shovel over glowing coals. Prepared this way the cornbread was known as "hoecake." In 1776 Benjamin Franklin wrote that hoecake was better than a Yorkshire muffin!)

Note: Elongated oval shapes can also be formed. My young son David says these shapes remind him of corn-on-the-cob.

CHICKEN (OR TURKEY) HASH

3-4 tbsp. margarine or vegetable oil
2 tbsp. flour
1 small onion, chopped
1 1/2 c. water
Salt and pepper
2 c. cooked chicken or turkey, chopped

    Heat the margarine or oil in a large skillet, and blend in flour. Add water. Slowly pour in water, stirring to thicken. Season with salt and pepper ". . . according to the taste of the man of the house," as one 17th century recipe directs. Add poultry, and simmer for 15-20 minutes. This may be served in a bowl as is; or over toast, cornbread, or waffles.

MIDDAY MEAL

The colonial midday meal was served anywhere from 2:30 until 4 p.m. The diversity and quantity of foods presented at that meal were staggering -- truly it was a "groaning board." (Of course, this was largely an agrarian society. The men and boys engaged in the vigorous physical labor of farming on a daily basis, and the "weaker sex" also managed to burn plenty of calories carrying out the none-too-easy chores of kneading bread, washing clothes by hand, scrubbing floors, spinning, etc. Therefore, when not fighting a war, the average affluent colonial citizens grew an abundance of food and individually ate their fair share of it.)

The midday meal might consist of soup; roast beef, roast pig, ham, or mutton (with gravy) or fish on Fridays; then another course: chicken, duck, wild game, or turkey; jams, jellies, and/or cranberry sauce; cakes, cookies; sweetmeats; puddings (Indian pudding, bread pudding, and plum pudding were all popular), and/or pies, and cheeses. Large cups of coffee were served throughout the meal. Cabbage or salad greens were often cooked with beef or pork, and sometimes a modern-type green salad accompanied the meat. (In the summer, crayfish salad was popular.)

Individual vegetables were beginning to receive attention in cookbooks by the mid-1700's. (Up until then they were frequently used as garnishes or ingredients in "made" dishes.) Mrs. Hannah Glasse, in her <u>Art of Cookery Made Plain and Easy</u>, advises: "Most people spoil garden things by overboiling them. All things that are green should have a little crispness, for if they are overboiled they neither have any sweetness or beauty."[1] Cooks were instructed to use minimal amounts of water in cooking vegetables. Field peas, sweet potatoes, pumpkin, squash, and corn on the cob were all well-liked. The influence of the much-admired French civilization was already being felt in the area of food preparation (even before the French became Colonial allies in the American Revolution). Cookbooks presented the English style of serving asparagus: cooked asparagus on toast with melted butter alongside in a boat [container]; and a French way: cooked asparagus with a sauce of egg yolks and vinegar (similar to Hollandaise sauce). Another approach was to scoop out the center of French rolls and fill them with creamed asparagus, replace the top of the roll, and fry the whole thing in butter. Mrs. Glasse wrote in 1714 in her <u>Art of Cookery</u> that broccoli could be served with "Butter in a Cup." She adds that "the French eat Oil and Vinegar with it."

Also by the mid-1700's the French style of table service was used here by the educated, wealthy families. The hostess carved and served one of the large meats on her end of the table and the host carved and served a "balancing" haunch of meat at his end. The table was laid out with platters and bowls of food arranged to achieve symmetry. No floral centerpieces were used -- instead a huge pie meat or a mock turtle (a fanciful arrangement of a cooked calf's head served on a real turtle shell; a ball of forcemeat -- similar to stuffing -- was positioned between the calf's ears, forming "the crown of the turtle"), or perhaps a joint of venison graced the center of the table. The "rule" was that if there were 12 diners, there should be 9 different dishes in each course. If there were 18 guests, 15 different dishes were required. (Family dinners were more conservative; 3, 4, or 5 dishes were acceptable per course.) Wine, beer, tea, or milk were offered as beverages in addition to coffee.

Onion soup (what we now refer to as "French" Onion Soup) was served in colonial days, as was Oyster Stew. Here are up-to-date recipes for these two favorites.

FRENCH ONION SOUP

1/4 c. butter
5-6 cups onions, thinly sliced
3 cans beef broth
Worcestershire sauce to taste
1/4 tsp. salt
French bread, sliced
Parmesan cheese

Sauté the onions in melted butter, until the onions are soft and slightly browned. Add beef broth, Worcestershire sauce, and salt. Bring to a boil and reduce heat. Meanwhile, toast French bread; top with Parmesan cheese. Lightly brown the bread with cheese under the broiler. Serve with soup, or floating on top of soup.

OYSTER STEW

2 tbsp. all-purpose flour
2 tbsp. water
1 tsp. salt
1 tsp. Worcestershire sauce [optional]
Dash of bottled hot pepper sauce
1 pt. shucked oysters, undrained
1/4 c. butter or margarine
1 qt. milk, scalded

Blend flour, water, and seasonings in a large pot. Add undrained oysters and butter. Simmer and stir gently over low heat 3 or 4 minutes. Add hot milk; remove from heat and cover. Let stand 15 minutes. Reheat briefly and serve. Serves 4 or 5.

After soup, the colonial diner could select from a buffet-like spread of meats. (Of course, one person did not eat large portions of everything. -- There were usually many children in a family, and often additional visiting relatives and friends also were present at the long table, so a variety of foods were offered from which the large number of people could choose.)

Smoked hams were popular. Following is a simple recipe to prepare today's more typical and affordable "picnic":

BAKED HAM

Double wrap ham in foil. Put in pan and bake at 400° F. for 30 minutes per pound.

Another well-known entree was Chicken Pot Pie, although older recipes delete the vegetables.

CHICKEN POT PIE

3-4 c. cooked chopped chicken
1 16-oz. can mixed vegetables, drained
1 can Cream of Chicken soup

```
1 c. chicken broth
1 c. self-rising flour
1 tsp. baking powder
1 c. milk
1/2 stick [1/4 c.] margarine, melted
```

Place chicken in a large casserole dish, and add vegetables, soup, and broth. Mix together, in a separate bowl, the next 4 ingredients for the topping. Pour the topping mixture over the chicken. Bake at 425° F. for about 45 minutes.

Note: Legend has it that George Washington and his fellow delegates to the Virginia House of Burgesses were served another "chicken classic" -- chicken salad. It seems that George Washington slept a lot of places and liked a lot of different foods!

As mentioned earlier, Continental soldiers were instructed to boil their meat for health reasons, but if the likelihood of official inspection seemed remote, the soldier enjoyed experimenting with other cooking techniques. Excavations of Revolutionary War campsites have brought forth bent pieces of strap iron (from old barrel hoops) fashioned to make broilers; and ramrods were said to have made excellent spits for broiling meat over the campfire.

The suffering and cold and deprivation of Valley Forge is well-known and documented. For the record, though, little snow fell in 1777-78, as compared to many a Pennsylvania winter. However, survival in pitiful housing and shortages of food made that winter a "time that tried men's souls."

Lt. Col. Henry Dearborn wrote, "This is Thanksgiving Day. . . but God knows we have very little to keep it with, this being the third day we have been without flour or bread. . . Upon the whole I think all we have to be thankful for is that we. . . are not in the grave with many of our friends."[2]

Private Joseph Martin, commenting on the same Thanksgiving, wrote with some sarcasm, "There was a

Continental Thanksgiving ordered by Congress... our country, ever mindful of its suffering army, opened her sympathizing heart so wide upon this occasion as to give ... each and every man half a gill of rice and a tablespoon full of vinegar!"[3]

Twenty-seven-year-old Dr. Albigence Waldo (surgeon in the ranks from Connecticut) recorded in his diary the daily menu at Valley Forge, "Fire cake and water, sir. . . The Lord send that our Commissary of Purchases may live on fire cake and water till their glutted guts are turned to pasteboard."[4]

Later, toward Spring, God intervened and the starving men were blessed with an unusually early and heavy run of shad up the Schuylkill River. As soon as the soldiers noticed the crowded-together fins of the fish rippling the surface of the water, the men plunged into the river armed with pitchforks, shovels, broken branches, and baskets to capture the shad. Other men ran for barrels and salt to store the surplus. When it seemed likely the shad would escape upstream, Major Henry Lee's dragoons charged into the Schuylkill, milling their horses around and forming a barrier. A long stretch of the river was thick with squirming fish -- a Godsend to the Continental soldier at Valley Forge.

It is recorded that baked shad was one of George Washington's favorite dishes, perhaps because of the important part that food played in the Valley Forge experience.

If a soldier was reminiscing about the delights of home, and mentally reviewing the possible menu of the day, his mind would list, after the soup and meat, a poultry course, perhaps a green vegetable or starchy vegetable, and then jams, jellies, possibly cheeses, and desserts.

Mrs. Hannah Glasse, the cookbook authoress, would approve of the following technique of preparing string beans (or green beans or snaps) so that they are not "overboiled":

STRING BEANS

1 1/2 lb. beans (pole beans are especially good)
Water

Remove ends and strings from beans. Put beans in a pot with a small amount of water. Bring to a boil, reduce heat, and cook for 15 minutes. Season lightly with salt. Serves 4-6.

Next is a recipe for corn pudding, a favorite of Gen. Daniel Morgan:

CORN PUDDING

4 large ears fresh corn
2 eggs, beaten
1 tbsp. butter, melted
1/2 tsp. salt
1/4 tsp. pepper
1 tsp. sugar
1 c. milk

Grease a 2-quart casserole dish. Cut top of kernels off corn, and then scrape the cob. (You should have 2 cups of corn.) In a bowl, add the remaining ingredients to the corn. Mix. Pour into the casserole. Bake at 400° F. for approximately 30 minutes or until puffy and golden brown on top. Makes 4-6 servings.

Besides all the other foods, in the South a bread called Sally Lunn might be served at dinner. This recipe was probably just coming into vogue around the time of the American Revolution. Folklore tells us that Sally Lunn was a pastry cook in the fashionable English resort of Bath. She peddled her tea cakes from a basket on the street until a baker named Dalmer bought her out, and began delivering hot "Sally Lunns" from portable ovens carried about in wheelbarrows.

SALLY LUNN

1 pkg. active dry yeast
1/4 c. warm water
1/2 c. hot milk
2/3 c. butter or margarine, softened
2 tbsp. sugar
3/4 tsp. salt
2 c. plain flour
2 eggs, well beaten

Dissolve the yeast in warm water. In a separate bowl, pour hot milk over butter, sugar, and salt. When the butter has melted, stir in 1/2 c. flour. Beat until smooth. Add the yeast mixture; mix well. Add half of the remaining flour and beat until no lumps remain. Add eggs; beat hard. Add remaining flour and beat vigorously at least 5 minutes. Scrape down batter from the sides of the bowl. Cover the bowl, and allow to rise in a warm place until doubled in size -- about 45 minutes.

When doubled, beat again at least 5 minutes, and then spoon into a greased 1 1/2-quart ring mold or Turk's head mold. Cover and let rise again until doubled.

Bake at 350° F. for 30-35 minutes, or until golden brown. Yield: one ring loaf.

Marblehead Pudding was a side dish served with roast pork, chicken, or turkey. [Col. John Glover had organized a group of fishermen from Marblehead, Massachusetts into a fighting unit. They managed the boats in the retreat from Long Island, and in the capture of Trenton. Perhaps this colonial accompaniment was named in honor of these heroic seamen.]

MARBLEHEAD PUDDING

1 c. molasses
1 tsp. baking soda
2 1/2 c. flour

```
Pinch of salt
1/2 c. water
3 tart apples, finely chopped
```

   Combine molasses and baking soda. Mix with flour and salt. Add water and apples. Put in a pudding pail and steam 2 hours. Serves 6.

Another favorite of the 18th-century citizen was strawberry preserves. In fact, when settlers first arrived here, they were amazed at the size and abundance of wild strawberries.

STRAWBERRY PRESERVES

```
4 cups strawberries
5 cups sugar
```

   Mix and let stand unrefrigerated overnight. Put in saucepan and bring to a rolling boil. Boil gently for 8 minutes. Add a scant 1/3 cup lemon juice. Boil 2 more minutes. Remove from stove. Skim. Let stand overnight or until thoroughly cooled. (Shake occasionally.) Pack in sterilized jars and seal or refrigerate in jars.

   The American colonists enjoyed sweets, and one of the well-known favorites was gingerbread. This cake, which originated in medieval Europe, was part of the standard diet for both Continental soldiers and redcoats during the Revolutionary War. (Later, in 1784, Mary Ball Washington served mint juleps and gingerbread to her son George and the Marquis de Lafayette. The availability of gingerbread to troops and spectators on Muster Day -- usually the first Tuesday in June, mhen military-age men met on village greens to drill and fire weapons -- became an enthusiastically-kept tradition.

   Another popular sweet of the day was Jumbles. Also spelled Jumbals, these cookies could be shaped in various ways depending upon the stiffness of the dough. They could be dropped [as in the following recipe], or rolled out and cut with a fluted cookie cutter, or shaped into a rope and tied into a knot.

JUMBLES

Cream the following:
    1 c. butter
    1 c. sugar
Add:
    1 egg
    2 tbsp. brandy or milk
    1/2 tsp. vanilla
    2 c. all-purpose flour
    1 tsp. ground cinnamon
    Raisin or nut halves [optional]

Drop on ungreased cookie sheet. Place a raisin or nut in center of each. Bake at 375° F. about 10 minutes. Makes 48.

Fudge has been made in the U. S. for almost 300 years. Here is a modern recipe to commemorate that delicious tradition:

FUDGE

1 stick margarine
4-5 tbsp. milk
1/4 c. cocoa
1 tsp. vanilla
1 box powdered sugar
3 tbsp. peanut butter (optional)
1/2 c. chopped nuts (optional)

Mix ingredients, except sugar, in a saucepan. Bring to a boil. Pour into a bowl containing the powdered sugar. Mix. Spread into a greased square or rectangular pan. Press down to make the top of the fudge level. Chill. Cut into squares to serve.[5]

Old recipes for cheesecake seem unbelievably rich, as seen in this recipe from E. Smith's Compleat Housewife, printed in Williamsburg in 1742. [This was the first cookbook published in America. William Parks of Williamsburg edited it from an earlier English work by Mrs. E. Smith.] This old recipe does not contain cream cheese.

LEMON CHEESECAKE

1/2 lb. butter
1 lb. sugar
2 lg. lemons, plus the grated peel
A dozen eggs
4 or 5 spoonfuls of cream

Combine ingredients and bake in a pastry shell. [The all-purpose pie crust of the 18th century was puff paste.]

UPDATED CHEESECAKE

2 small packages cream cheese
1/3 c. sugar
1/2 tsp. vanilla
1 egg, slightly beaten
1 9" graham cracker crumb crust
1 cup of sour cream

Cream together cream cheese, sugar, vanilla, and egg. Put into the crumb crust and bake at 325° F. for 20 minutes. Hike the oven up to 450° F., spread a cup of sour cream all over the top of the pie, sprinkle a tablespoon of sugar on that, and bake it for 5 minutes.

Note: For a more healthful dessert, substitute mock sour cream for the dairy sour cream. The mock sour cream is made as follows:

In a blender combine 1 c. cottage cheese and 1 tbsp. lemon juice. Blend until smooth.

Another old-fashioned treat is cottage cheese pie. (It is so good and nutritious you could serve it for breakfast!) Mrs. E. Smith had a version of cottage cheese pie back in 1742, but this recipe takes advantage of modern ingredients and conveniences.

COTTAGE CHEESE PIE

2 c. cottage cheese
2 egg yolks
3/4 c. sugar
1/4 tsp. salt
1 pkg. (3 oz.) egg custard mix
1/4 tsp. lemon juice
2 tsp. vanilla
3 tbsp. melted butter
3/4 c. milk
2 egg whites, beaten stiffly
1 9-inch unbaked pastry shell

Blend together the first four ingredients. Add the next five. Lastly, fold in egg whites. Pour into the pie shell, and bake at 325° F. for 30 minutes.

Apple Brown Betty is a less complicated dessert, probably more popular among the ordinary folk than the aristocracy. Its simplicity makes it perfect for today's tastes.

APPLE BROWN BETTY

2 c. soft bread crumbs
1/4 c. margarine
3 c. apples, sliced (they need not be peeled)
1/2 c. sugar
1 tsp. cinnamon
3/4 c. water

Saute bread cumbs in margarine. Add apples, sugar, cinnamon, and water. If the skillet is oven-proof, cover and put in oven. If the skillet is not oven-proof, transfer apple mixture to a greased casserole dish. Cover and

bake at 375° F. for 30-40 minutes, until apples
are translucent and tender. If mixture becomes
too dry during baking, add 1/4 cup water.
(Apples vary as to moisture content.) This
will serve 4 or 5 people.

Ice cream has been around for a long time. In 1744, William Black was traveling with the Virginia commissioners for the Lancaster treaty with the Iroquois. He stopped off in Annapolis, Maryland. There Gov. Thomas Bladen, whose wife was French, entertained him and his companions. One of the "Rarities" served at dinner was "some fine Ice Cream."[6] Following is an old-fashioned recipe for some fine apricot ice cream.

APRICOT ICE CREAM

12 ripe apricots, peeled, stoned, and puréed
    (other fruit can be substituted)
6 oz. sugar
1 pt. scalding cream

    Combine ingredients. Place in a tin or pewter container in a tub of ice and salt. (Some cooks stirred the ice cream as it hardened, others didn't.)

To imagine more abundant food than the "typical" colonial dinner is difficult, but at Christmas and on special occasions all the stops were pulled out (what a stark contrast to the soldiers' meager camp fare!). "Before Dinner comes on the Table" at Christmastime an appetizer of raw oysters "laid in their Shells in a Dish" or thin slices of a pickled collar of meat were presented.[7] A possible third course, wedged in someplace after the meat courses, was nuts and fruits served on a bare table. At this time toasts were drunk.

"Spirits" were indeed well-liked by 18th-century citizens -- but, of course, genteel people did not overindulge. Syllabub and wassail were two beloved holiday beverages (in addition to the wines, brandies, punches, toddies, etc.).

SYLLABUB

This is an ancient English recipe. Originally the froth on top was achieved by placing the punch bowl filled with wine and seasonings directly under a cow's udder and milking. The air bubbles on top created the froth. It was then served immediately -- not chilled. (Today this frothy effect can be achieved with the addition of egg whites.) The taste of syllabub is similar to eggnog.

2 c. cream, cold
2 c. milk, cold
1/2 c. sherry
1/4 - 1/2 c. sugar
Few grains of salt

Beat all ingredients with a rotary beater until the sugar is dissolved and the mixture is bubbly. Pour into 8 cups and sprinkle generously with nutmeg.

Note: The wine used to make Syllabub in the colonial period was from Sillery, France, and "bub" meant a bubbly drink in England; hence, "Syllabub."

WASSAIL

Wassailing is an extremely old English custom, part of the feasting associated with New Year's. A bowl of spiced ale was offered to the master of the house who drank to the health of all present. After that the bowl was passed around and each individual present drank, and repeated the Saxon phrase "Wass hael," which means "be whole" or "be well." The following modern recipe is for those who prefer a non-alcoholic beverage.

3 c. boiling water
1 family-size tea bag
2 c. sugar
1 qt. cranberry apple juice (or 1 pt. cranberry juice and 1 pt. apple cider)

```
1 1/2 tsp. cinnamon
1/2 tsp. cloves
1 1/2 c. orange juice
1/2 c. lemon juice
```

   Steep the tea bag in the boiling water for
5 minutes. Remove the tea bag. Add sugar,
cranberry apple juice, and spices. Simmer 5
minutes. Add citrus juices. Heat to simmering.
Serve hot. (This punch can be prepared, stored
in a glass jar, then reheated.)

   A favorite at Christmas, fruit cake was also enjoyed
by our colonial ancestors. The following is a composite
of the ingredients of four 18th-century recipes, demonstra-
ting the variety of components used in a typical fruit
cake. [A <u>rich</u> fruit cake recipe of the day called for
4 lbs. flour, 4 lbs. butter, 2 lbs. sugar, 30 eggs, and
the usual fruit, nuts, spices, and brandy <u>for one cake</u>.]

```
1 lb. butter
1 or 2 lb. sugar
Dozen eggs
4 lb. raisins (or half currants)
1 lb. citron
1/2 lb. lemon peel (or half orange peel)
1 lb. blanced almonds
1/2 lb. figs
1/2 lb. cherries
3/4 lb. dates
1 lb. walnuts
Spices:
     allspice
     mace
     nutmeg
     cinnamon
     cloves
     ginger
1 c. molasses
1 c. brandy (or a pint of sherry)
1 glass currant jelly
Flour to make a stiff batter
```

   The next recipe is a current rendition of the classic
fruit cake.

20TH CENTURY NO-BAKE FRUIT CAKE

1 box vanilla wafers, crushed
1 box graham crackers, crushed (or the
    equivalent amount of packaged graham
    cracker crumbs)
1 c. candied red cherries
1 box white raisins
1 box dark raisins
2 pkg. figs, chopped
2 pkg. dates, chopped
2 c. mixed nuts (pecans, Brazil nuts, English
    walnuts)
1 lg. bag marshmallows
1 can Eagle Brand condensed milk

Note: Save out some cherry and nut halves to decorate the top of the cake.

Combine the first eight ingredients. Meanwhile, in a double boiler, melt the marshmallows into the condensed milk. Add this mixture into the dry ingredients, a little at a time, until moist. Pack this mixture into a cake mold lined with wax paper. Arrange the extra cherries and nuts on top of the cake in a pretty pattern. Wrap well with plastic wrap, and store a few weeks in refrigerator before using.

Turning our attention from the gala and extravagant holiday fare of the non-fighting citizen to refocus on the Continental soldier, we look again at that legendary winter of desolation at Valley Forge. 11,000 of Washington's men were encamped at Valley Forge, in hastily constructed log cabins (hardly more than shacks). 3,000 men died in camp from disease, cold, and starvation. Over 500 rotting horse carcasses polluted the camp, the beasts having died from hunger, "for want of forage."[8]

Subsequently Gen. Washington appointed Nathanael Greene as the new Quartermaster General. This hard-driving man was better able to get food and clothing to the troops. Greene's motto became "Forage the country naked!" His raiders confiscated cattle; or killed them, rather than let the British get them later.

Even with more intensive foraging, though, suffering was still a problem. On April 12, 1780, Gen. Washington noted not "one ounce of meat fresh or salt in the Magazine." On April 14 only bread was available for the army.

We study recollections of James Collins, a sixteen-year-old American rifleman who helped wipe out 1200 Loyalists on King's Mountain in October 1780. Collins recalled, "Everyone ate what he could get [as the backwoodsmen headed for the mountain between the Carolinas] and slept in his own blanket, sometimes eating raw turnips and often resorting to a little parched corn. . . ."

After a victorious battle Collins awoke the next morning to the sad scene of Tory wives and children coming to see if their man was dead or alive. Collins reports, "Their husbands, fathers, and brothers lay dead in heaps, while others lay wounded or dying. . . We proceeded to bury the dead, but it was badly done. They were thrown into convenient piles and covered with old logs, the bark of old trees and rocks, yet not so as to secure them from becoming a prey to the beasts of the forest, or the vultures of the air; and the wolves later became so plenty, that it was dangerous for anyone to be out at night for several miles around. Also the hogs in the neighborhood gathered into the place to devour the flesh of men, inasmuch as numbers [of people] chose to live on little meat rather than eat their hogs, though they were fat."[9]

SUPPER

How the Continental soldier longed for peace! And yet, for the cause of liberty, he chose to fight on, against seemingly impossible odds for eight grueling years. As Patrick Henry had declared in 1775, "Is life so dear, or peace so sweet, as to be purchased at the expense of chains and slavery? Forbid it, Almighty God! I know not what course others may take, but as for me, give me liberty, or give me death!"

It could be said that the Continental army's best "peacemakers" in dealing with the British were the Brown Bess (the standard flintlock smoothbore musket of the redcoats, but also used by Americans), the French Charleville musket, and the Pennsylvania rifle. In New Orleans another kind of Peacemaker, called "La Médiatrice," has been favored for years. It is a deluxe sandwich consisting of fried oysters in a French bread loaf. The recipe is akin to one found in Mrs. E. Smith's Compleat Housewife, published in London in 1739. (In the 1742 Williamsburg edition of the Compleat Housewife, the cook was instructed to use a little nutmeg and some bread crumbs along with the eggs, salt, and flour for batter for frying oysters; and then to fry them in beef drippings.) Below are the directions for preparing a "Peacemaker" -- minus nutmeg and beef drippings.

LA MÉDIATRICE/PEACEMAKER/OYSTER LOAF FOR TWO

1 pint shucked oysters, well-drained
2 eggs
1 c. yellow cornmeal (or all-purpose flour)
1/2 tsp. salt
1/4 tsp. pepper
Vegetable oil
1 loaf French bread
2 tbsp. butter, melted
Mayonnaise
Bottled hot pepper sauce
Catsup or cocktail sauce
Lemon wedges

Pat the drained oysters dry with paper towels. In a small bowl beat the eggs. In another bowl mix the cornmeal or flour, salt and pepper. Dip the oysters in the beaten egg; coat

with flour mixture. In a saucepan or deep fryer
heat about 2 inches of oil to 365° F. Fry the
oysters, a few at a time, for 2 minutes or until
golden. Drain on paper towels.

Slice the French loaf in half lengthwise;
brush with butter. Heat in a 350° F. oven for
about 5 minutes. Arrange the oysters on the
bottom half of the loaf. If desired, spread the
cut side of the top half with mayonnaise. Sprinkle
the oysters with hot pepper sauce. Cover with the
top half of the French bread. Serve hot with
catsup or cocktail sauce and lemon wedges.

Oyster loaf would have been enjoyed by colonial
diners as a supper dish. After their ample breakfasts
and mammoth noon meals, a simpler repast was served
around 9 or 10 p.m. (Other possible "feeding times"
included Ladies' Afternoon Tea -- a "snack" of bread and
butter, hot buns, crumpets or muffins, cake, and tea
partaken of by some gentlewomen; and the grand Ball
supper -- an extravagant dessert course held at midnight
during a dance.)

For the family supper a dish of seafood (oysters
were well-loved) or a cold meat were usually served; or
"battered eggs"; and bread, butter, and cheese; fruit; a
light dessert; and wine or cider.

A highly favored colonial supper dish (or a second
course at the midday meal) was Salmagundi. Legend has it
that Marie de Medici, wife of France's Henri IV, was fond
of a snack of minced veal, chicken or turkey with pickled
onions or herring and boiled eggs, all chopped and served
with oil. The story continues that Marie combined the
first and last names of a lady-in-waiting to form the word
"salmagundi." A less entertaining explanation is that the
French word is derived from the Italian term for salted
meat, "salame conditi."

Today we would call the 18th-century concoction a
chef's salad. Possible ingredients then included assorted
salad greens, ham, turkey or chicken, anchovies or pickled
herring, hard-cooked eggs, cheddar cheese, celery, parsley,
black olives, garnished with capers. Other components of

the salad might be cucumbers, apples, onion, gherkins, watercress, pickled red cabbage, and nasturtium flowers. Often this "antipasto" was arranged over an inverted bowl, creating a dome effect. A bit of shaped butter was placed on top of the salad, and one was advised to "have a small glass with egg mixed as for sallad, to eat with the salmagundi"[1]; or it could be served with oil and vinegar dressing. This was, and is, a recipe to get creative with!

Early accounts of life in Virginia tell of the mammoth crabs found in Virginia waters. These fine creatures measured a foot in length and six inches across, and were said to furnish an adequate meal for four men. To celebrate the still-magnificent Chesapeake crab, here is an outstanding recipe for crab cakes.

CRAB CAKES

1 lb. crabmeat, flaked (check for bits of shell)
1 tsp. Old Bay seasoning
1 tbsp. mayonnaise
1 tbsp. Worcestershire sauce
1 tbsp. chopped parsley
1/4 tsp. salt
1 tbsp. baking powder
1 egg, beaten
2 slices of bread, crumbled
Milk (enough to moisten bread crumbs)

Mix all ingredients and shape into 8-10 round crab cakes. Sauté lightly in butter or oil in a skillet over medium heat. Cook briefly, turning once. Allow 2 crab cakes per person.

In the swirl of activities surrounding the Revolution, we see how the Continental soldier subsisted and what his normal diet would have been had he not been in the army. We see how French cuisine took on new appeal to the colonists (as did any form of cooking that did not smack of the strong-handed British government and the redcoats and Tories who represented it). Since the cuisine of the colonies was essentially borrowed from the British Isles (with a few colonial "originals" such as cornbread, baked pumpkin, and succotash developed to utilize native American ingredients), the Patriots were quick to see the irony of eating Banbury tarts while fighting the English. Certain foods found that their names were suddenly changed from English Plum Pudding to American Plum Pudding, or from English trifle to merely trifle. As the war dragged on, no doubt anything labeled "English" fell into greater and greater disfavor. After Cornwallis surrendered, American life was decidedly less British, and this difference was obvious in the already rapidly changing American diet. The influence of African cooking reached a slave-owner's table via his black cook; tourists to and from European countries exchanged recipes -- the newborn country was literally becoming a culinary melting pot.

It might be extrapolated that the ease with which the colonists accepted new styles of cooking reflected their readiness to embrace new ideas and accept change and innovation -- all part of the charm and success of this nation. As Benjamin Franklin wrote prophetically to George Washington, "I must soon quit the Scene, but you may live to see our Country flourish, as it will amazingly and rapidly after the war. . . Like a field of young Indian Corn, which. . . by a Thunder Gust of violent Wind, Hail, and Rain seemed to be threatened with absolute Destruction; yet the Storm being past, it recovers fresh Verdure, shoots up with double Vigour, and delights the Eye not of its Owner only but of every observing Traveller."[2]

FOOTNOTES

INTRODUCTION

1. Bart McDowell, <u>The Revolutionary War</u>, Washington, D. C., National Geographic Society, 1967, p. 60.

2. Charles K. Bolton, <u>The Private Soldier Under Washington</u>, New York, 1902, pp. 78-79, quoted in Harold L. Peterson, <u>The Book of the Continental Soldier</u>, Harrisburg, Pennsylvania, The Stackpole Company, 1968, p. 146.

3. Bolton, pp. 80-81, quoted in Peterson, p. 146.

BREAKFAST

1. Richard M. Ketchum, Editor, <u>The American Heritage Book of the Revolution</u>, New York, American Heritage Publishing Co., Inc., 1971, p. 149.

2. C. C. Pinckney to Moultrie, May 24, 1778, William Moultrie, <u>Memoirs of the American Revolution</u>, 2 volumes, New York, 1802, Vol. I, p. 213, quoted in Peterson, p. 142.

MIDDAY MEAL

1. Hannah Glasse, <u>The Art of Cookery Made Plain and Easy. . .By a Lady</u>, 7th ed., London, 1760, p. 18, quoted in Jane Carson, <u>Colonial Virginia Cookery</u>, Williamsburg, The Colonial Williamsburg Foundation, 1985, p. 45.

2. Ketchum, pp. 217-218.

3. Ibid.

4. Albigence Waldo, <u>Valley Forge, 1777-1778, Diary</u>, printed in <u>Pennsylvania Magazine of History</u>, XXI, 1897, quoted in Milton Meltzer, <u>The American Revolutionaries: A History in Their Own Words 1750-1800</u>, New York, Thomas Y. Crowell, 1987, p. 119.

5. Recipe provided by Mrs. Max Carter, Morganton, North Carolina.

6. "Journal of William Black, 1744," Pennsylvania Magazine of History and Biography, I (1877), p. 126, quoted in Carson, p. 136. The following recipe, "Apricot Ice Cream," is from Elizabeth Whitaker Raffald, The Experienced English Housekeeper, for the Use and Ease of Ladies, Housekeepers, Cooks, etc., 1st Edition, Manchester, 1769, pp. 249-250, quoted in Carson, p. 110.

7. Sarah Harrison, The House-keeper's Pocket-book, and Complete Family Cook. . ., 6th Edition, London, 1755, quoted in Carson, p. 4.

8. McDowell, p. 130.

9. James P. Collins, Autobiography of an American Soldier, 1859, p. 149, quoted in Meltzer, pp. 150-151.

SUPPER

1. Carson, p. 104.

2. McDowell, p. 195.

PATRICIA B. MITCHELL FOODWAYS PUBLICATIONS

REVOLUTIONARY RECIPES

COOKING FOR THE CAUSE

SOUTHERN BORN AND BREAD

TRUE GRIST

HEARTH RISE YEAST BREADS

GOOD THINGS COME IN SMALL BREADS

DELIGHTFUL NIGHTS OF DIXIE DINNERS

A MONTH OF MAGNIFICENT MAIN DISHES

MY HEART'S IN NEW ORLEANS
                BUT MY SUPERMARKET ISN'T

SOUTHERN SPECIALTY VEGETABLES AND SALADS

SIMPLY SCRUMPTIOUS SOUTHERN SWEETS

NOW, THAT'S SOMETHING TO CROW ABOUT

SWEET 'N' SLOW

WELL, BLESS YOUR HEART, Volumes I and II

from the

Historic Sims-Mitchell House